Minute Help Guides Presents:

A Newbies Guide to Word 2013 RT

SOME PEOPLE ONLY HAVE A FEW MINUTES TO SPARE

Minute Help Guides

Minute Help Press

www.minutehelp.com

Table of Contents

Introduction

In the 22-odd years since the company unveiled their suite of productivity programs, Microsoft Office has become synonymous with *serious* computer work. Whether it's a Fortune 500 conglomerate's all-important spreadsheet or a homemaker's recipe catalog, MS Office has been the dominant force in productivity applications for a very long time. While Apple, Google and their ilk have certainly created a competitive atmosphere in recent years, nobody can touch the usability, customization, or sheer power of the Microsoft Office suite.

Now, with the release of their first official tablet computer, Microsoft has upped the ante, optimizing and customizing Office for the touch screen powerhouse they've dubbed Windows RT. While a good chunk of the functionality that Office users have gotten used to over the years remains the same, there are a few new things to get acquainted with.

This guide will take you through the basics of Microsoft Word, the most popular desktop publishing application ever released. We'll show you what you need to get started, everything from creating and saving your documents (with SkyDrive) to turning your finished documents into blog posts or sharing directly with friends and colleagues. Whether you've been using word processing applications for years, or you're still clinging to your old Smith Corona typewriter, we'll not only show you how to craft perfect documents, we'll have fun doing it!

At a glance, Word RT 2013 looks like an incredibly complex program. It *can* be, but it definitely doesn't *have* to be. This guide will teach you what you need to know to get to work *right now*, leaving the fluff and the head scratching for people with time to waste.

Ready to get started? Let's go!

Part One: Getting Started with Word RT 2013

First Things First: Supported Devices, Keyboard Covers, and Other Accessories

Before we dive right in, there are a couple of things we'll need to discuss to make sure you're able to get the most out of Office RT. While this guide is primarily geared toward Surface RT users, Microsoft has licensed the software to a few other hardware companies, which means that you *could* be using any one of these other devices:

- Asus VivoTab RT
- Dell XPS 10
- Samsung Ativ
- Lenovo IdeaPad Yoga (RT)

Office RT will function identically on these other devices, but this section will focus on peripherals you'll want to have for the Surface.

> *Note: Microsoft has released two different versions of the Surface tablet, one labeled Surface RT and one labeled Surface Pro. Since the Surface Pro is essentially a full-fledged computer shoved into a tablet form factor, they do not include <u>any</u> version of Office with it. Office RT is, in fact, a specially coded version of the software meant to be used with what's called ARM processors – chips used primarily in mobile devices. The Surface Pro uses standard X86 chips, which makes it 100% incompatible with Office RT. Long story short: if you bought a Surface Pro, you'll have to buy your own copy of Word, which will have a slightly different set of features than the version discussed in this guide.*

Covers –

While the Surface RT doesn't automatically ship with a keyboard, Microsoft has engineered two different, equally elegant solutions: the 'touch' cover and the 'type' cover:

The touch cover is not really a keyboard, at least not exactly. It's an incredibly thin, touch-sensitive mat, with a keyboard layout. Completely flat to the touch, typing on it can take a little getting used to. The type cover is more akin to a regular keyboard – the keys have a fair bit of 'travel', which means they move when you press down.

Either solution is perfectly suitable, depending on your preferences, but we highly recommend picking one up. An on-screen keyboard is fine for web browsing or jotting down small notes, but you're definitely going to need a real keyboard to get anything bigger accomplished. Both of these keyboard covers are available for around $120 – the rest of this guide will assume that you've got one.

Both of these keyboard covers also come with a built-in trackpad, which functions in the same way that a laptop trackpad does. For those of you that dislike trackpads, we also recommend picking up a USB mouse. Hundreds of them are compatible with the Surface RT, but if compatibility isn't specifically listed on the model you'd like to pick up, check out www.microsoft.com/compatibility to be sure. A whole lot of devices are compatible, even ones you'd *never* think were. Case in point: Apple's Magic Multi-Touch Trackpad works flawlessly, according to the compatibility check:

Apple Magic Multi-Touch Trackpad
MC380LL/A

Available for:

Windows 8	Windows RT	Windows 7		Compatibility status may vary by operatin

Apple

Homepage   Support   Contact

The Magic Trackpad is the first
multi-touch trackpad designed to
work with your Mac desktop ...

Show more...

Model	Status		Community ratin
MC380LL/A	✓	Compatible No Action Required	Compatible : **3** Votes Not compatible : **0** Votes

Give us your vot

Compatible	Not comp

The same goes for printers. While all three of the printers in our office were compatible, it's a good idea to check the website before getting frustrated when you *need* to print a document right away and can't.

WYSIWYG: A Quick Word Primer

If you're already familiar with Microsoft Word and/or the WYSIWYG (What You See is What You Get) paradigm, feel free to skip this section entirely. For the uninitiated among you, let's take a quick minute to discuss what *exactly* Word RT is and what the program can do for you.

In the days before computers were a constant presence in virtually every home, normal people who needed to create documents did so with typewriters. When a mistake was made, there were two choices: start over, or break out the Whiteout. Though the typewriter was revolutionary in every sense of the word, it was really only good for the simplest of communications – a letter, a memo, or similar "small" tasks. More complicated layouts – newspapers, magazines, brochures, etc., were next to impossible to create for anyone but the most experienced professional, working with expensive (and dangerous!) tools to *cut and paste* the appropriate items into a readable format.

Somewhere in the early 90s, everything changed. Home computers became increasingly common – and increasingly powerful—at an astounding pace. By the mid-90s, the average 12 year old could create something on a home computer that would've taken an entire team of design editors at The New Yorker weeks or months to craft just a few years earlier. The concept of "desktop publishing" democratized the once difficult task of creating professional-level documents, making it easier and easier for *everyone* to participate. Desktop publishing's rise mirrored the rise of the Internet, giving birth to citizen reporting, blogging, and every other participatory aspect our wired world enjoys today.

Microsoft was at the forefront of this revolution. Over just a few years, Microsoft Word evolved from a simple, somewhat clunky "virtual typewriter" to a full-featured text production powerhouse:

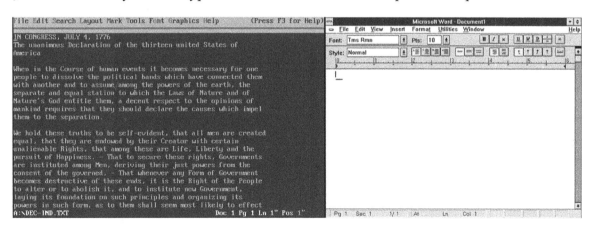

In fact, the picture on the left is taken from a version of Word released just 3 years before the one on the right.

Now, the concept behind Word has been refined over the years, but it remains as simple and as bold an idea: With Microsoft Word, you can create all manner of documents, everything from a simple letter to a complete and properly formatted novel. You can change typefaces and add pictures, illustrations, footnotes, and headers – basically anything you can do with text, you can do it with Word. Everything you create within the program will come out looking *exactly* as you've created it, whether it's a screenplay, a blog post, or an entire web page. We really can't stress this enough: the only limit is your imagination.

Word's biggest strength is in its review process: Word can automatically look for mistakes in spelling, grammar, and formatting, allowing you to correct anything that needs correcting before finalizing and/or printing a document. It's basically like having a full-time, professional editor/assistant at your fingertips. And, luckily for you, Word RT 2013 is the most advanced version of the software ever created.

It might seem a little complicated at first, but that's only because of the sheer number of useful features the program contains. We'll go over everything you need to get accustomed to it throughout this guide, but first let's get the boring setup stuff out of the way, shall we?

Updating/Finalizing Office RT

As you may have already noticed, Windows RT devices shipped with a 'preview' version of all the Office RT apps. Luckily, it's a snap to update it to the final version. According to Microsoft, this update should happen automatically, but that wasn't the case in our experience – we actually attempted an automatic update three times before we gave up. Have no fear, though; Just follow these simple steps to get yourself updated.

> *Note: For some reason, this update doesn't cancel out the original 'preview edition' completely. If you ever have to reset your RT device back to factory defaults, you'll have to go through this update process again. We're not sure why, but it's something you may have to deal with in the future.*

To get started with updating, just bring up the charms bar by swiping right to left. Once you've done that, tap the 'settings' charm:

Once you've done that, you'll be taken to the settings menu, which will look something like this:

To find the update menu, tap 'Change PC Settings'. This will bring up the more advanced menu, which will look like this:

Tap 'Windows Update' to continue. Once there, tap the button labeled 'Check for Updates'. After a few moments, you'll find a list of updates that Microsoft wants to apply. Go ahead and tap 'Install' and let it do its work. Depending on the number of updates that are found, this could take a little while. Trust us; it's worth the hassle to stay updated.

Once you've applied all the updates, your Office apps should no longer be labeled 'Preview' and should look like this on the Home Screen:

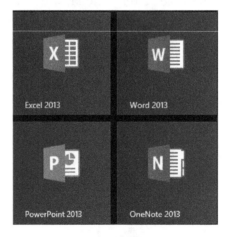

That's all there is to it. We're almost ready to dive right in, there's really only one more thing to set up: SkyDrive.

Your Documents in the Cloud: Setting up SkyDrive

Over the last few years, you've probably heard about "The Cloud" and its impact on computing. If you don't know any better, it sounds sort of scary and complicated. Rest assured that it's not. "The Cloud" is really just a buzzword – it's shorthand for online storage and nothing more. How does this relate to your Windows RT tablet?

If you're like most people, you probably have a few internet-connected devices lying around. You might use your desktop computer for some things, while other tasks are relegated to your smart phone or tablet. All these different gadgets are great for getting stuff done, except in one crucial way: how do you get your stuff from one device to another? How do you keep everything organized and up to date? Microsoft's answer to that is SkyDrive, and it's a great solution.

Microsoft has included 10 GB of SkyDrive cloud storage with every Surface tablet, while users of the other Windows tablets we discussed earlier will only have the 7 GB that comes for free. Users of cloud storage services like Dropbox or iCloud will be familiar with the concept behind Microsoft's SkyDrive, but the company's take on it is a little bit different, especially for Windows RT tablets.

Basically, SkyDrive is a folder (or group of folders) stored on the Internet, but accessible only to you and your devices. Copying a file from your computer to SkyDrive will make the file available instantaneously across all of your other SkyDrive-enabled devices. Setting up SkyDrive on your PC is crucial, especially if you use Office on devices other than your Windows RT tablet.

For example, let's say you've written a document in Word on your PC. You're sitting in the living room, watching television, when you suddenly remember a paragraph or two you've forgotten to include. You can just pull the same file up on your Surface tablet and edit it without having to trudge back to your home office. The changes you make from the living room will automatically be applied to the file on your PC.

> *Since this guide will primarily focus on working with Word RT, perhaps a better example would be creating a document on your Surface tablet, and then saving it to SkyDrive for later use.*

To get started, we'll have to download the SkyDrive application to whichever devices you'd like. In Windows 8 or on your Windows RT tablet, that's as easy as searching for the app in the App Store and downloading it. If you're using another operating system, like OSX, Windows 7, or Windows Vista, it's a little bit more complicated.

To download the application, head over to www.microsoft.com. Once there, you'll notice a search bar in the upper right hand corner. Type 'SkyDrive' in the search bar and click search. The first result will be the SkyDrive app. Click again to download it.

Once it's downloaded, click to open the file and install it. Follow the prompts and enter your Microsoft ID and password in the fields. Make sure it's the same ID you use on your Windows RT device. That's all there is to it. You'll now have a folder on your desktop that looks like this:

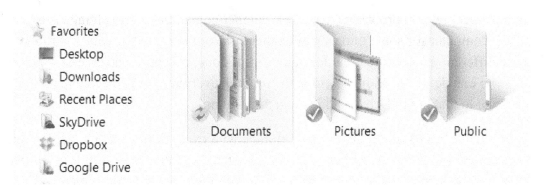

Copy whatever you like to it: documents, music, videos, etc. Whatever you copy will almost instantly appear within the SkyDrive app on your Windows RT tablet:

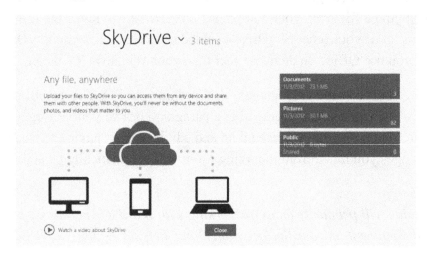

As a special bonus to users of Windows 8, installing SkyDrive will allow you to synchronize the settings of all of your Windows 8 and Windows RT devices. Your tile layout, background, system settings – all of it will match up perfectly if you want it to. Of course, you always have the ability to opt-out of that. For more info on Live Tiles and customization, consult "The Newbies Guide to the Microsoft Surface Tablet", available at www.minutehelpguides.com or from any major online bookseller.

Now that you've set up the SkyDrive app, you can share the files on your Surface to it. It's as easy as swiping in the charms bar and tapping Share:

To make it even easier, Word RT has a built-in SkyDrive solution. Simply tap to save the document you're working on and (after installing it on your Windows RT device) SkyDrive will appear as an option:

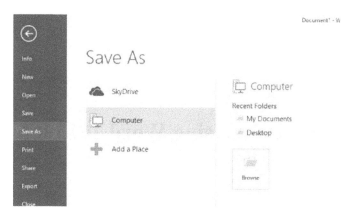

But, let's not get ahead of ourselves. In the next section, we'll begin to learn the basics and find our way around the program.

Ready? Let's go!

Part Two: Using Word 2013 RT

Navigating Word RT 2013 – The Basics

To get started with Word RT, let's go ahead and open the program. This can be done in one of three different ways. Unless you've removed the Office icons from your Start Screen, you'll find the Word RT icon there, right alongside the other Office applications. Just tap it to open the program. Alternately, you can swipe up from the bottom to bring up the 'All Apps' listing and find Word RT there. Yet another option would be switching your tablet to 'Desktop' view and tapping the Word icon in the bottom left corner of the screen. However you get there, once you've opened the program for the first time, you'll be presented with this screen:

This is Word's Start Screen. You'll begin here whenever you open Word RT, unless you start the program by opening a specific document, which we'll discuss a little later. As you can see, there is a space on the left for recent documents, and once you've used the program and saved a document or two, your most recently opened documents will appear here for quick access. There are also a bunch of templates to choose from, but for now just tap (or click, using your tablet's keyboard trackpad) the item labeled "Blank Document" to open a new—you guessed it—blank document.

Once you've done this, you'll be presented with a new Word document, represented by the white space in the middle of the screen:

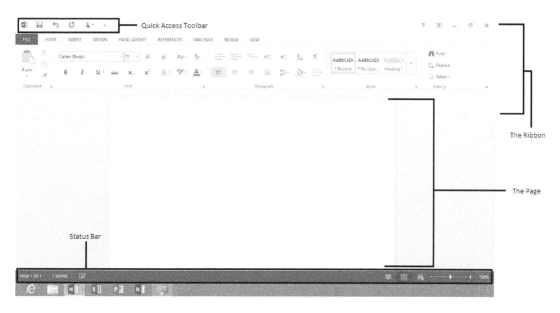

As you can see from the illustration above, Word RT 2013 is comprised of several different areas. What we've dubbed "The Page" is your document. Everything within this area is a part of it. Above that area, you'll find what's referred to as "The Ribbon". The Ribbon area contains all of the things you can *do* to the page. This is where we'll make changes to the layout and style of our document. We'll go over The Ribbon in detail a little later in this guide.

Entering and Formatting Text

On the page, you'll see a blinking cursor. This represents where you are on the page. All of the text you enter will appear to the right of this, until you reach the end of a line, at which point you'll start fresh on a new one.

From here, you can begin typing whatever you'd like. By default, Word RT will capitalize the first word after a period, and continue in one long paragraph until you hit the enter key. Tapping enter will begin a new paragraph. As you can see in the above illustration, you can quickly change the way your text is presented by tapping any of the most common styles:

B – This represents bold. Anything you type after pressing this will **look like this.** Tap (or click it) again to turn off bold. This is useful for titles and paragraph headings, or for added emphasis.

I – Tapping this will turn your words into *italics.* This is commonly used for emphasis and titles. Again, tapping or clicking a second time will revert to normal text.

<u>U</u> – Tapping here will underline text.

~~ABC~~ - While slightly less common, tapping this will turn your words into ~~strikethrough.~~ This comes in handy for corrections.

X_2 and X^2 – These, known as subscript and superscript, are mainly used for annotating – including bibliographies, references, and footnotes.

> *There are keyboard shortcuts for most of these commands – and a whole lot more. Check out the shortcuts section near the end of this guide for a list of the most useful ones.*

Just above these buttons, you'll find two boxes that look like this:

These boxes allow you to select the font type (on the left) and the font size (on the right). There are dozens of different fonts to choose from, everything from Broadway to Verdana, which gives you a quick way to customize your documents. Just tap or click the arrow to bring up a list of potential fonts, and tap or click the arrow next to the size to change the size of the text.

Now, stopping to change the way your text looks every time you'd like to change something can get tedious. With that in mind, there's a simpler way. As an example, we typed out the first few paragraphs of the Herman Melville classic "Moby Dick" without stopping to change anything:

```
Moby Dick

By Herman Melville

Call me Ishmael. Some years ago--never mind how long precisely--having
little or no money in my purse, and nothing particular to interest me on
shore, I thought I would sail about a little and see the watery part of
the world. It is a way I have of driving off the spleen and regulating
the circulation. Whenever I find myself growing grim about the mouth;
whenever it is a damp, drizzly November in my soul; whenever I find
myself involuntarily pausing before coffin warehouses, and bringing up
the rear of every funeral I meet; and especially whenever my hypos get
such an upper hand of me, that it requires a strong moral principle to
prevent me from deliberately stepping into the street, and methodically
knocking people's hats off--then, I account it high time to get to sea
as soon as I can. This is my substitute for pistol and ball. With a
philosophical flourish Cato throws himself upon his sword; I quietly
take to the ship. There is nothing surprising in this. If they but knew
it, almost all men in their degree, some time or other, cherish very
nearly the same feelings towards the ocean with me.

There now is your insular city of the Manhattoes, belted round by
wharves as Indian isles by coral reefs--commerce surrounds it with
her surf. Right and left, the streets take you waterward. Its extreme
downtown is the battery, where that noble mole is washed by waves, and
cooled by breezes, which a few hours previous were out of sight of land.
Look at the crowds of water-gazers there.
```

As you can see, we neglected to properly format the title and author portion at the top. It's an easy fix. To format areas that you've already passed, just highlight the area you'd like to change by clicking at the beginning or end of the area, holding, and then dragging your finger until the rest of the area is covered. This is called highlighting. Notice the background color of the area you selected has changed. Once you've done that, just right click to bring up the text options menu:

From here, you can change the font, the size, or add bold, italics, create a list, or anything else you see. These are not your only options, however. Every option in the Ribbon can also be used. Clicking will change the formatting to whatever you've clicked, but only for the text you've selected:

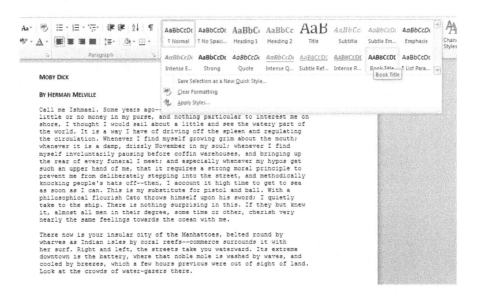

Aside from clicking and dragging to highlight, there are a few other shortcuts to selecting and highlighting text:

- To highlight a single word, position the cursor anywhere in the word and double-click.
- To highlight an entire sentence, hold down the Ctrl key and then click anywhere in the sentence.
- To highlight a paragraph, triple-click anywhere inside the paragraph.

Once you've highlighted text, you can also move it around manually. This is referred to as 'drag and drop' and is a quick way to move text a short distance. To do this, simply click and hold the selected text, move it where you'd like it, and then let go. It might take you a few tries to get the hang of it, but it's a lot more convenient than cutting and pasting for small jobs.

Quick Access Toolbar

Above the ribbon along the left hand side you'll find the Quick-Access Toolbar. By default, this area will contain several items, from left to right:

- The minimize/maximize/close button – tapping or clicking here will allow you to make the program take up more (or less) screen space, or also close it entirely. If there have been changes made to the document since the last time it was opened, you'll be asked if you'd like to save any changes before the program closes.
- The save button – allows you to save your document whenever you like with one tap (or click).
- Undo – tapping here will reverse the last thing you did with your document. This includes words added, font changes, and any formatting changes you may have done. Tapping (or clicking it) multiple times will continue undoing things one step at a time.
- Repeat – tapping or clicking here repeats the last action. This is useful for formatting and/or recreating text boxes and things of that nature, which we'll go over a little later.
- Touch/Keyboard – this is a toggle. By tapping here, you can switch from a layout optimized for touching with your fingers, or one better suited for use with a keyboard and mouse. The 'touch'

portion spreads out the items on the Ribbon, so that they're easier to tap. We'll discuss this further in the next section.

Directly next to the 'Touch/Keyboard' toggle, you'll find another button. By tapping here, you can customize what is displayed on the Quick Access Toolbar. There are dozens of different commands and combinations to choose from. It's all up to you, but in our case, some of the more useful things to add here were:

- Spell Check – tapping this will immediately run through the spelling and grammar check for the whole document.
- Print Preview/Print – obviously only applicable if you've installed a printer to use with your Windows RT tablet.
- Increase/Decrease Font Size –this is useful when you're trying to make sure a certain amount of text fits on a specific page.

We'll go over a few more of these over the course of the guide, but we'll leave it to you to figure out what works best for your workflow. Many people aren't even aware of this customization option, and thus never miss it.

The Ribbon at a Glance: File and Home

In the last section, we touched on some of the common functions that the Ribbon interface serves. In case you haven't noticed yet, the Ribbon is the nerve center of the Word RT universe. Everything you can do with Word can be done from here. Of course, all these buttons and icons can be a little unnerving, especially to the average Office newbie. In this section, we'll take the mystery out of the Ribbon and show you how to find what you need and ignore what you don't.

By default, the Ribbon will be optimized for use with a keyboard. All the functions and icons will be a little condensed, and thus difficult to tap with your fingers. It's a good idea at this point to switch to the slightly easier to deal with touch version, which will look like this:

To do that, simply tap the button on the right side of the Quick Access Toolbar and tap 'Touch.' Even though we're working with a keyboard, it helps to have a little extra space.

Now that we've adjusted the view, let's take a deeper look at the Ribbon. You'll notice that the Ribbon is divided into 9 different groups: File, Home, Insert, Design, Page Layout, References, Mailings, Review, and View. Each offers a different set of options for your document. By default, Word will remain in the Home area, which is where all the text formatting we've previously discussed resides. It's a good idea to stick with the Home view while writing, but each different group contains some important elements. Let's take a look at the two you'll be spending the most time in: File and Home.

File

This area contains the high-level options and information for both your current file and the entire Word RT program. From here, you can save, print, and share your document. This is also where you'll head to close the program, or open a new or existing document.

Along the left hand side, you'll notice several menu options. The expanded information will appear on the right, depending on which menu item is selected. The items are:

- Info – this contains all the information about your document. Things like the date and time the document was created, who the author is, size, and number of pages. If you've edited the document more than once, this is also where previous versions will be stored. You can access a previous version of the file at any time without erasing the work you've already done. From here, you can also inspect the document for any formatting issues. Some previous versions of Word aren't 100% compatible with Word 2013 files. We'll talk about that a little later in this guide.

- New – clicking this item will bring up the Word RT 'Start Screen' we discussed earlier. From here, you can create a new document, either blank or by using a template. Recent documents are also visible from here.
- Open – clicking this item will allow you to choose an existing Word document to open. You can choose from recently accessed documents, or bring up the file browser to find the one you're looking for.
- Save – clicking here will save the document wherever you choose. If you haven't saved the document yet, you'll be sent to the Save As menu item automatically.
- Save As – clicking here will allow you to save the document in any of the various supported formats. We'll discuss document formats a little later in this guide.
- Print – clicking here will bring up the print options, allowing you to set up the document for printing.
- Share – clicking here will bring up the sharing options for your document. There are some pretty cool options here, which we'll discuss at length in the "Presenting, Sharing, and Blog Posting" section of this guide.
- Export – Word RT has built-in support for PDF (Portable Document Format) files. From here, you can create a PDF that will be viewable by anybody, even those without access to Microsoft Word. We'll go over this in the "Saving, Converting, and Printing Documents" section of this guide.
- Close – tapping here will close the currently open document.
- Account – there's a lot of information in this menu item, most of it centered on all of the services you might use with Word RT. Any of the social networks you've signed up for with your Windows RT tablet will be visible from here, as well as your Microsoft account details. You can also change (or remove) the photo that accompanies your Microsoft account from here, which can be useful if you plan on using Word RT's sharing functions for any professional-type work. More on that later.
- Options – this menu item is a shortcut to the general Word RT options menu. This is where you'll change the username and/or initials associated with your documents, as you can see in this illustration:

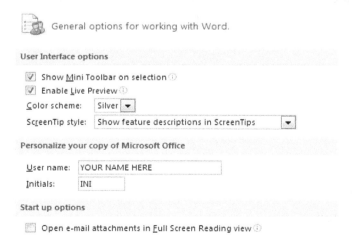

Home: Cut, Copy, Paste

As we've discussed already, the Home section of the Ribbon is where you'll probably be spending most of your time while working in Word RT. As the default Ribbon view, we've already shown you that the Home section contains most of the options you have for changing the way your text looks, but there are a few other important things to note.

First, let's talk about cut, copy, and paste. These functions, named somewhat esoterically after the physical actions a graphics person would undertake before the advent of digital publishing, cutting, copying, and pasting are absolutely vital to your Word RT experience. But what exactly do they do? Let's find out.

- Cut – this action will remove a selection from your document, placing it *temporarily* in your computer's memory, usually to be placed in a different location shortly thereafter.
- Copy – this action will copy a section of your document (or a web page, picture; anything that can be placed in your document), while leaving the original in place.
- Paste – this action will place the previously cut or copied selection into your document.

Confused? Don't be. It's simpler than it sounds. As an example, let's say that you've written a letter. Everything you want to say is included, and you're basically done. While proofreading, you notice that your letter would make more sense if the third paragraph was actually the second. Rather than deleting what you've done and retyping the paragraph, you can just cut (or copy) it and paste it where it actually belongs. Just highlight the area using any of the methods from the last section, and then click (or tap) the scissors icon on the top left of the Home Ribbon to cut, or the two pieces of paper icon below it to copy:

Once you've cut or copied your selection, move the cursor to where you'd like to place the content and tap the icon labeled 'Paste'. That's all there is to it.

Of course, you can also right-click anything you've highlighted to bring up a context menu with the same options:

The great thing about right-clicking is that it works in many other programs, most notably Internet Explorer, where you can copy a chunk of text (or an image) and paste it into your document in the very same way.

One other important thing to note: when you copy an item to your clipboard, it will become the default thing to paste once you decide to, but everything else you've copied during a writing session is still saved in the clipboard. To access the *other* stuff you've copied, just click arrow to the right of the word Clipboard, which is just below paste:

Once you do that, you'll bring up the Clipboard Pane, which will have everything you've copied into the clipboard during your writing session, including text and photos:

To paste one of these items into your document, just tap or click on it. That's all there is to it.

Home: Find, Replace, Select

The other important area of your Home Ribbon is all the way to the right. This is where you'll encounter the Find and Replace functions, as well as a handy shortcut to making various complex selections.

- Find – clicking here will allow you to search for a word (or a string of words) within your document. This is useful for longer documents, or for just checking out how often you're using a particular word.
- Replace – clicking here will allow you to replace a word (or string of words) with another word.
- Select – clicking here will bring up options for selecting various things in your document – everything from the entire document, to *just* the images can be selected from here.

****

Review

Spelling and Grammar

As you've no doubt noticed by now, Word RT has a pretty sophisticated built-in spelling and grammar checking system. Whenever you see a wavy line underneath a word or series of words, the program has detected a possible flub on your part. Some of the more common spelling errors are even automatically corrected as you type. For example, try typing the word misspell with only one 's'. Did you notice how it automatically corrected the word? This happens with a lot of very commonly misspelled words, including "a lot", which is the preferred spelling of the dreaded "alot" . Pretty cool, huh?

Let's take a closer look at how all of this works.

Now, when you type a word that the program believes is misspelled, it's generally for one of two reasons: either you've mistyped the word, or Word RT is unfamiliar with it. This can often happen when typing newly created words like Copernicum (a recently discovered element) or with new products, like the Windows RT tablets we mentioned at the beginning of this guide:

- Asus VivoTab RT
- Dell XPS 10
- Samsung Ativ
- Lenovo IdeaPad Yoga (RT)

Once you've identified a word that isn't misspelled, but still registers as such, you have a couple of options. One, you can ignore it (and everything else Word RT may find) until you've completed your document. You can run a thorough spell check at any time. This will take you through each and every spelling and grammar issue, one by one, throughout the entire document. You can start a spelling and grammar check in two different ways. First, you can click to the Review tab on the Ribbon. Once there, you'll find an icon that looks like this:

Simply click (or tap) the checkmark to begin. Word RT will automatically begin proofreading your document from top to bottom. If you'd only like to proofread a certain section of the document, just highlight that section and *then* click the checkmark.

This function is duplicated at the bottom of your document in the Status Bar area. Click the icon that looks like this to perform the same function:

*If your current document has no spelling or grammar errors, there will not be a red 'X' on this icon, which can serve as a nice visual clue that everything is correct.

Once you begin the proofreading, Word RT will show you everything it identifies as a mistake. This will take the form of a dialog box that will look something like this:

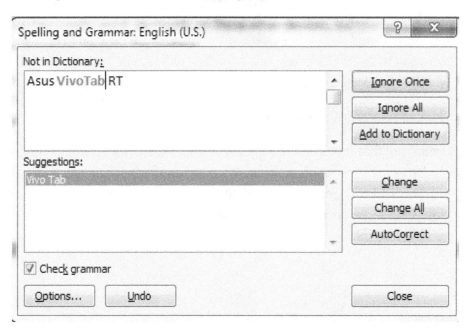

As you can see, Word RT found our not-actually-misspelled word VivoTab. We have several different actions to choose from here. The actions at the top right will all keep the word as-is:

- Ignore Once – selecting this will move on from the word, ignoring it in just this one instance. If the word is repeated later in the document, you'll have to choose again.
- Ignore All – selecting this will ignore every instance of the word within the document.
- Add to Dictionary – selecting this will add the word to Word RT's internal dictionary, which will make sure the word is never misidentified as misspelled again.

The three options on the bottom right will, by contrast, change the word:

- Change – selecting this will change the word to the highlighted word in the center. Sometimes, there will be several suggestions, so make sure the correct suggestion is highlighted.
- Change All – selecting this will change *all* instances of the word within the document to the highlighted suggestion.
- AutoCorrect – selecting this will automatically change the offending word to the correction *as you type*, eliminating the need to spell check. It's basically the same function as our earlier 'mispell' test.

For this particular instance, we selected the 'Add to Dictionary' function. Once we've done that, the word will remain as it was in the original document, only this time without the pesky red line beneath it:

- Asus VivoTab RT
- Dell XPS 10
- Samsung Ativ
- Lenovo IdeaPad Yoga (RT)

As you can see, however, we're still left with a few other unfairly underlined words in this little chunk of text. We could go on with the spelling and grammar check, but let's discuss a simpler way to correct these issues as they arise.

Once Word RT has underlined a word, you can right click it to bring up an options menu. This serves as a sort of simplified spell check, which will offer suggestions and give you the very same options as the full-fledged document-wide spell check:

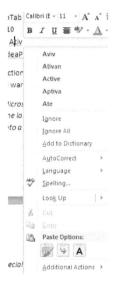

As you can see in the illustration above, we're offered a bunch of potential corrections for the word "Ativ" as well as the option to ignore or add to the dictionary.

Now, lest you think that these tricks are only useful for words that aren't actually misspelled, the system works wonders for the occasional typo and brain-freeze too:

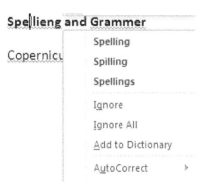

So that covers misspelled words, but what about grammar? Word RT has you covered there too. You may or may not have noticed some other squiggly lines, either in green or in purple. Green is used to signify a problem with an entire sentence, like so:

Now, in this case, Word RT is assuming that this sentence isn't a sentence at all, but a fragment, an incomplete thought. While this isn't actually the case for this sentence (the subject, you, is implied), Word RT isn't taking any chances. You can correct these kinds of errors in the very same way as a spelling error:

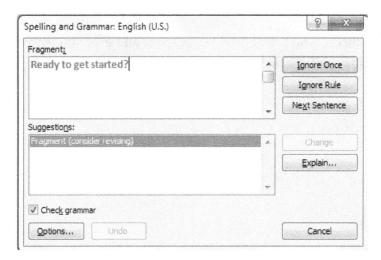

- Ignore Once – selecting this will ignore the fragment one time.
- Ignore Rule –selecting this will stop Word RT from noticing these potential errors
- Next Sentence – selecting this will just skip to the next potential error
- Change – generally, Word RT won't suggest changes to sentence fragments, so this is usually not selectable
- Explain – selecting this will give you a brief overview of the grammar rule(s) that resulted in the potential error.

Just like with spelling errors, you can take these on one at a time by right-clicking to find the same basic options.

The third, and arguably most complex type of error that Word RT is capable of finding involves words that, while not misspelled in a technical sense, aren't appropriate for the sentence they're being used in. This is usually a case error, like "their, there" or "its, it's" or something similar. It can also be something as silly as the difference between Chile (the country) and chili (the delicious food item). Here's an example:

Your a Wizard, Harry!

Now, "Your" is obviously a real word. But in this case, we're actually supposed to use "You're" the contraction instead. These small errors happen all the time, and are exceedingly difficult to catch on your own. People just whiz right past them because they're not technically misspelled.

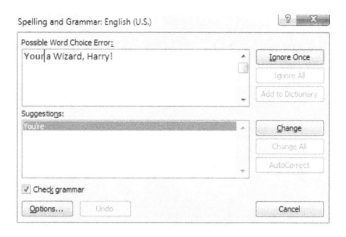

Now, we probably don't need to tell you that Word RT's proofreading function, amazing at it is, is not a *perfect* substitute for real-world proofreading. If your document absolutely has to be perfect, nothing beats a second (or third) set of eyes for catching mistakes. Not even a computer!

Inking and Highlighting

All of this spelling and grammar check wizardry is great, but it's by no means the only way to correct text. Word RT contains two of the most important mistake correcting tools every invented: inking and highlighting. While these two things will be instantly familiar to anyone who has ever taken an English class, this high-tech update will (at the very least) keep the smudges away from your fingers. Let's take a quick look, shall we?

So, what exactly does inking and/or highlighting do? It's simple. They are digital versions of your teacher's famous red (or green, or blue) pens and highlighters. You can use them to highlight areas that need work, questions for any collaborators who might later see the file, and so on.

To get started with inking and highlighting, click on the review tab of the Ribbon menu. On the right hand side, you'll see an icon that looks like this:

Click the icon to begin. Once you've done that, you'll be presented with the inking and highlighting menu in the same place the Ribbon would normally be:

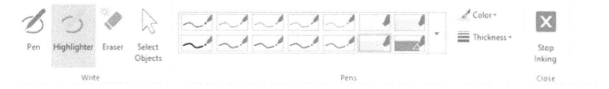

From here, all you need to do is choose your tool. Pen for inking and highlighter for highlighting. Choose whatever color and thickness you'd like, and then try it out on your page. Just click and drag anywhere on the page you'd like to highlight. Your results will look a little something like this:

Moby Dick

By Herman Melville

Call me Ishmael. Some years ago--never mind how long precisely--having little or no money in my purse, and nothing particular to interest me on shore, I thought I would sail about a little and see the watery part of the world. It is a way I have of driving off the spleen and regulating the circulation. Whenever I find myself growing grim about the mouth; whenever it is a damp, drizzly November in my soul; whenever I find myself involuntarily pausing before coffin warehouses, and bringing up the rear of every funeral I meet; and especially whenever my hypos get such an upper hand of me, that it requires a strong moral principle to prevent me from deliberately stepping into the street, and methodically knocking people's hats off--then, I account it high time to get to sea as soon as I can. This is my substitute for pistol and ball. With a philosophical flourish Cato throws himself upon his sword; I quietly take to the ship. There is nothing surprising in this. If they but knew it, almost all men in their degree, some time or other, cherish very nearly the same feelings towards the ocean with me.

There now is your insular city of the Manhattoes, belted round by wharves as Indian isles by coral reefs--commerce surrounds it with her surf. Right and left, the streets take you waterward. Its extreme downtown is the battery, where that noble mole is washed by waves, and cooled by breezes, which a few hours previous were out of sight of land. Look at the crowds of water-gazers there.

Now, if you'd like to remove a highlight or an inking, just click the eraser and make the same clicking and dragging gesture. It's that simple. To exit inking mode, just tap the icon labeled 'Stop Inking'. That's all there is to it. Anyone who views your document will see your highlights and/or red pen marks, which is super handy when collaborating with one or more people.

Of course, your documents will still print normally, without the highlights and ink, unless you *want* them to. We'll get into that when we discuss printing a little later in this guide.

Dictionary and Thesaurus

The last parts of the Review Ribbon we need to concern ourselves with are no less important than the others, and far more important for some. Word RT has a built-in thesaurus and dictionary system, indispensible for writers of term papers, or really anyone who needs to sound a little smarter than average. Let's see how it works.

To save space on your Windows RT tablet, Microsoft doesn't exactly include the dictionary with Word; the dictionary needs to be downloaded first. Don't fret, though: it's easy and it'll only take seconds.

To download your dictionary, all you need to do is tap (or click) the dictionary icon, which is located on the top left of the Review Ribbon, just to the right of the Spell Check icon:

Once you've selected the dictionary, a pane will open to the right of your document:

There are several options to choose from here, including several generic dictionaries, a Merriam-Webster version and Microsoft's own Bing Dictionary. We recommend selecting the Bing Dictionary, as it appears to be the highest rated and most-often updated of the bunch. Whichever you choose, however, just click the 'Download' icon that corresponds. Depending on your Internet connection, it might take a few minutes to complete, but once it has, go ahead and click the 'x' in the upper-right corner of the dictionary pane to close it out.

Now that your dictionary has downloaded, you're almost done. Search for your first word now. Go ahead and highlight any word in your document, and then tap or click the Dictionary icon. Once you've done that, the dictionary pane will open up on the right. The first time you do this, it will look like this:

As usual, Microsoft errs on the side of caution when it comes to your privacy. Of course, there's nothing shady going on here, so just tap (or click) the start button to allow the dictionary access to your document. You'll only have to do this once. From now on, whenever you highlight a word and click the dictionary icon, you'll be greeted with something approaching this on the right hand side of your document:

Just like with spelling and grammar, you can also right click to bring up a context menu. To do this, just highlight the word you'd like to define, then right-click. You'll be presented with the context menu, only now you'll see an option labeled 'Define.' Just tap or click there to bring up the dictionary pane.

The thesaurus is another handy tool. Luckily, it doesn't need any setting up. It just works out of the box. If you'd like to find a potentially better word, or a word with the opposite meaning, just highlight the word and tap (or click) the icon directly below the dictionary icon. Once you've done that, you'll be presented with the thesaurus pane, which will look something like this:

Most words will have several synonyms to choose from and at least one antonym. To choose a different word, just double-click one of the suggestions and it will be automatically placed where the original was.

You can also use the same right-click context menu as with spelling and the dictionary. Just highlight the word, right-click and then select the menu item labeled 'synonyms' and choose a replacement word. It's that simple.

Part Three: Getting More out of Word 2013 RT

Now that we've covered the basics, let's dig a little deeper and begin discussing some more advanced concepts. Let's start by discussing the easiest way to customize your documents: templates and themes.

Ready? Let's roll.

Templates and Themes

At the beginning of this guide, we opened a blank document, ignoring the templates menu entirely. Now that we've learned a little bit about how Word RT works, let's revisit that opening menu and find out what this template business is all about, shall we?

Before we begin with templates, let's discuss exactly *what* a template is. In the simplest terms, a template is a blank document that's pre-formatted for a particular purpose. There are dozens upon dozens of different templates – everything from resumes to screenplays. With Word RT, Microsoft has significantly upped the ante with templates, giving you a handy template search function to find just the right starting point for your document. While you could spend hours crafting the perfect document, it's actually a heck of a lot easier to just find something that looks like what you'd like your finished product to look like and go from there. After all, you want to spend your time with Word RT getting things *done*, right?

To begin working with templates, click the File tab on your Ribbon menu. Once you've done this, click on the menu item on the left labeled 'New'. This will bring up the opening menu that we discussed at the beginning of this guide. This time, however, we're not going to create a blank document; we're going to find an interesting-looking template and click (or tap) on it to get a better view. As you can see, there's a search function at the top, but for now, let's just look through the default templates and find the one labeled 'Newsletter.' Click it to get a better view. Once you've done that, you'll see something like this:

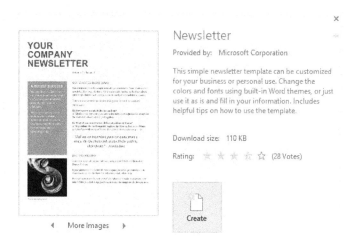

From here, you can see a little more information about the template, including a handy star rating and a description. To look for another template, click the x in the upper right hand corner of the template box. To begin working with the template, click 'Create'. For this example, we'll be working with this template, so go ahead and follow along by creating the template now.

Once you've done that, you'll be taken to your new document, which is full of the formatting and text of this template. The goal of any template is to replace what's called the "dummy" text with text of your own. To do that, just click anywhere and replace the dummy text with your own:

MOBY DICK'S NEWS

Volume 1 / Issue 1

WE NEED A BIGGER BOAT

You might use a sidebar for a

CATCHING THE ELUSIVE WHITE WHALE

You can just replace the sample text with your own for a clean, professional newsletter that's easy to share. Or if you want to customize the look, check out the tips that follow to help you create exactly the newsletter you want.

You can do the same with any pictures you see. Entire sections of the template can be deleted by simply selecting them and cutting, just like the cutting and pasting we discussed earlier. Remember that you can hit the back arrow at the top of the screen to reverse anything you've done, so feel free to experiment.

Now, this template is pretty straightforward and appropriate for any number of things, but the orange color scheme isn't exactly easy on the eyes. Don't worry about it: everything can be changed, while maintaining the professionalism. In fact, it only takes a couple of clicks. The color scheme and font style are collectively referred to as the theme. There are a few different methods for changing the theme of a template, all of which are easy as pie.

To get starting with changing the theme, click on the Design tab of the Ribbon. Once there, you'll be greeted with a Ribbon that looks like this:

You'll notice a dropdown menu labeled 'Themes' in the left hand corner. Click it to bring up a list of pre-made themes for the template. These are designed to look good together:

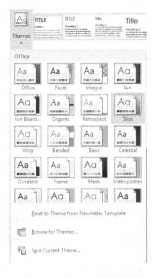

Click on any one of the themes to change to it. Again, you can always revert back, so don't be afraid. Click on any of the themes that strike you – we went with a blue theme that's easy on the eyes, but not too different from where we started:

MOBY DICK'S NEWS

Volume 1 / Issue 1

WE NEED A BIGGER BOAT

You might use a sidebar for a brief story about an important event or a company success story that you want to highlight.

This is also a great place to show off your mission statement or other content you want to highlight boldly in every issue, such as upcoming events.

[Click here to add a caption]

CATCHING THE ELUSIVE WHITE WHALE

You can just replace the sample text with your own for a clean, professional newsletter that's easy to share. Or if you want to customize the look, check out the tips that follow to help you create exactly the newsletter you want.

Think a document that looks this good is hard to create? Think again!

Q: How can you match the formatting?
A: All of the text formatting you see in this newsletter is just a click away! On the Home tab, check out the Styles gallery.

Q: What if you want to use different colors or fonts?
A: No problem! On the Design tab, explore the Themes, Colors, and Fonts galleries for a wide range of looks. Then just click to apply one you like.

"Call out an important point or quote from a story. On the Home tab, in the Styles gallery, click Quote." – Attribution

GET THE PICTURE

To replace a sample picture with your own, right-click it and then click Change Picture.

If your picture isn't a perfect fit for the space provided, you can crop it in almost no time. On the Picture Tools Format tab, click Crop.

Want to zoom in on the best part of your photo and make it stand out even more? After you click Crop, just drag to resize the image inside the crop area.

In addition to the new color scheme, you'll notice a subtle difference in the font style. While they are pre-made to look good together, you may want to change *just* the color or font style of a template. To do this, just click on either of the icons labeled 'Colors' and 'Fonts' to bring up the individual changes you can make:

Colors   Fonts

There are hundreds of different templates, though to save space, they aren't included in Word RT. That's the reason for that handy search bar at the top. Anything you might want is going to be there. Keep in mind that many of these templates are contributed by users just like you, so be sure to check ratings and descriptions to make sure you're not wasting your time on a low quality template. New templates are released on a constant basis, so we're pretty sure you'll be able to find something that fits your needs. Happy hunting!

Saving, Converting, and Printing Documents

Now that we've created a document, it's time to 'finalize' it. We do this in a few different ways. The first, and most obvious, is by printing. Creating a hard copy of your document is as easy as clicking the File Ribbon tab and clicking print. Once you do this, you'll be taken to the print menu. Toward the right will be a preview of your document. On the left, you'll see the print options, which will look like this:

Print

Copies: 1

Print

Printer

Ready

Printer Properties

Settings

Print All Pages
The whole thing

Pages:

Print One Sided
Only print on one side of...

Collated
1,2,3   1,2,3   1,2,3

Portrait Orientation

Letter
8.5" x 11"

Custom Margins

1 Page Per Sheet

Page Setup

Generally speaking, if you're not printing legal documents or birthday banners, nothing much will need to be changed here. Assuming that you've installed a printer, all you really need to do is click the printer icon on the top left. If you'd like to print more than one copy, change the number next to 'Copies'. If you only want to print a portion of your document, add the pages you'd like printed next to 'Pages'. That's really all there is to it. Consult your printer's guidebook if you have trouble.

Even after printing, your document still needs to be saved, if you ever plan to use it again. To do this, just click the File menu item labeled 'Save'. The first time you do this, you'll be automatically redirected to the 'Save As' menu. From there, you'll be asked to pick a place to save to. If you've set up SkyDrive, that will be listed as an option. We recommend saving to SkyDrive, as it'll be available for use on other devices. It's also a great 'just in case' strategy. After all, you never know when your tablet might fall into the ocean.

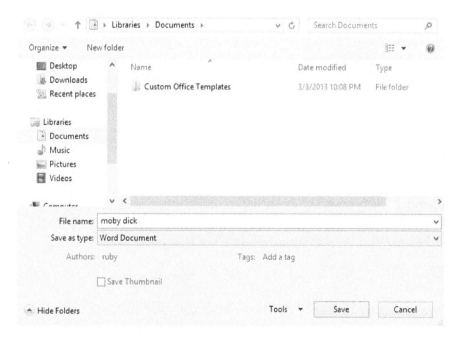

Once you've decided where to save your document, you'll be brought to the "save as" dialog box. Word RT will attempt to create a title for your document using the first line of it. In some cases, this is fine. In others, you'll want to change it:

To change the title of your document, just tap in the box labeled 'File Name' and replace the suggested title with your own. Once you've done that, pick the folder/location you'd like to save to and click 'Save'. That's all there is to it.

Notice that underneath the file name, there is another box labeled 'Save as Type'. As we discussed earlier, not everyone will be able to read a Word 2013 document. Thankfully, Microsoft has included support for a bunch of different file types. To change the file type (also known as converting), just click the arrow on the right side of the box. This will bring up a dropdown menu of supported file types:

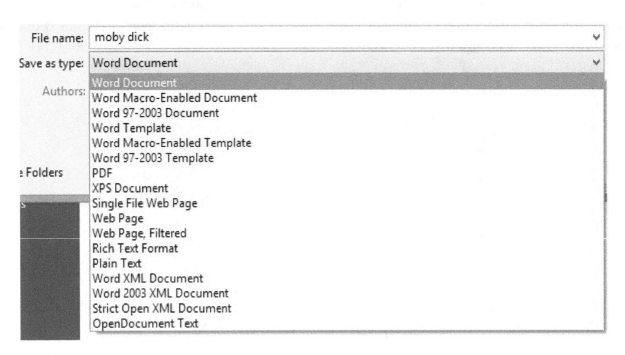

As you can see, there are an awful lot of options. Consult whoever else will be reading the document to figure out which would be the best. Bear in mind that some of these formats won't retain the same formatting as your document. Saving as either PDF or Word Document is generally the safest bet. In fact, you can do both by saving first as a Word Document, then repeating the process and saving as a PDF. Better safe than sorry!

Blog Posting, Sharing, and Social Networking

Now that we've learned how to save our stuff in various formats, you might think that's about all we can do with a completed document. To paraphrase every infomercial ever made, "But wait! There's more!"

By heading to the File menu, you'll see a menu item labeled 'Share'. This is where we'll do everything in this section of the guide. Go ahead and navigate there now.

Blog Posting

If you've been paying attention to the online world over the last several years, you've probably heard quite a bit of chatter about blogging. You may even have a blog of your own. Word RT actually integrates with most of the popular blogging platforms, allowing you to post *right* from the program. Pretty cool, right? Let's take a look at it.

To get started with blogging, click the menu item labeled 'Post to Blog'. You'll be presented with a screen that looks something like this:

From here, click the icon labeled 'Post to Blog' toward the bottom of the screen. Once you've done that, Word RT will send you back into your document, only this time it will be automatically formatted for blog posting. From here, you'll be asked to register your blog account:

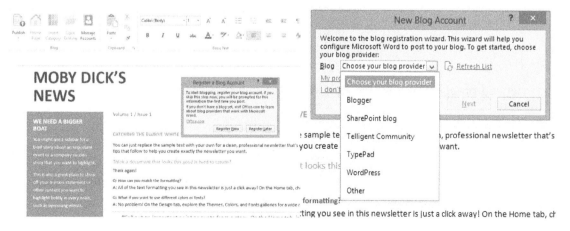

Click 'Register Now' and fill in the required info: your username/password and the URL of your blog.

Once you've done that, you'll be asked to confirm the privacy details. Accept, and then you'll be all set up for blogging. You'll be taken back to your document, only now there will be a 'Post Title' box at the top of it. Change this to whatever you'd like, as it will be the title of the blog post once it's published. Make any other changes you'd like to and then tap the icon labeled 'Publish' on the top left of the Ribbon:

That's it. Your blog has now been posted online:

For the experienced blogger, posting through Word RT can be a real time-saver.

Sharing

In addition to blogging, there are several other ways to share your document with other people. First, you can invite people to view your document. To do this, click on the 'Invite People' menu item. If you haven't yet, you'll need to save your document to SkyDrive before getting this set up:

Just tap the 'Save to Cloud' icon to get started, and save the document like you ordinarily would. Once you've done that, you'll be taken to a page that will allow you to enter the names of your contacts, or standard email addresses of people you'd like to share the document with.

By default, these people will be able to edit your document, make changes, and download it to their home computers. If you'd like to restrict their access to read-only, change the drop-down menu on the right side of the screen to read 'Can View' rather than 'Can Edit':

Below this, you're given space to enter a message for your recipients. Once you've entered all of that information, just click the 'Share' icon to send a link to everyone on your list:

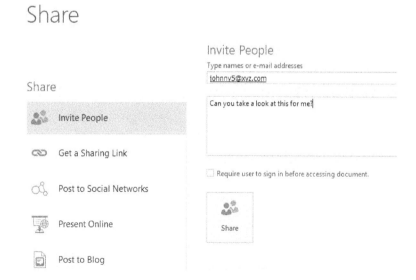

To bypass all that email sending, you can simply head to the next menu item. Labeled 'Get a Sharing Link,' clicking here will allow you to copy the URL (Internet address) where the file is located. Anyone you give this URL to will be able to access the document.

You're actually given two different links: one for people to view the document, and another for people to edit the document:

Social Networking

If all of the options we've just discussed aren't quite enough for you, Microsoft has also included automatic sharing to your social networks as a choice. Of course, you'll need to have connected your Windows RT tablet to your social networks to use this feature. If you've done that already, it's a snap to share this way. Just click the menu item labeled 'Post to Social Networks'. Once you've done that, you'll be presented with a menu that looks something like this:

As you can see, all of your connected social networks will appear with a checkmark next to them by default. If you'd only like to share to one social network, just tap the checkmark next to the one you don't want to remove it from the list. Much like the 'Share' option, you're given an option to allow people to edit (or just view) the document, as well as some space to add a message. Bear in mind that Twitter has a 140 character limit, so do your best to not be overly verbose.

Once you've made your selections, tap the icon labeled 'Post' at the bottom. Almost instantaneously, your document will appear on the selected social network(s):

As you can see, your contacts can interact with these posts in the exact same way as any other post you've made. They can reply, comment, like, favorite, or re-tweet what you've posted, depending on the network. Also bear in mind that *anyone* on your social networks can view this material, so sensitive documents should probably not be posted.

That's all there is to it!

Keyboard Shortcuts

While most every task we've discussed in this guide can be accomplished by finding the appropriate item in the Ribbon, stopping a frenzied writing session to change something can get pretty tedious after a while. These keyboard shortcuts, separated into groups of common (and some not so common) tasks, can be an incredible time saver once you get used to them.

> *While this list is not entirely comprehensive, it's made up of the shortcuts we use ourselves, shortcuts that we think will help you out. For a complete list of Word RT 2013 keyboard shortcuts, consult Microsoft's Office web site at http://office.microsoft.com.*

To use these keyboard shortcuts, just press the key combinations listed from left to right. For example, pressing and holding the Ctrl key and then pressing B will turn on **bold** type. Pressing that combination a second time will turn off bold type. The shorthand for this will be Ctrl+B, meaning Ctrl AND B, not Ctrl and + and B.

Opening and closing documents

- Create a new document   Ctrl+N
- Open a document   Ctrl+O
- Close a document   Ctrl+W
- Save a document   Ctrl+S

Working with text

- Toggle bold   Ctrl+B
- Toggle italics   Ctrl+I
- Toggle underline   Ctrl+U
- Increase font size   Ctrl+]
- Decrease font size   Ctrl+[
- Cut a selection   Ctrl+X
- Copy a selection   Ctrl+C
- Paste selection   Ctrl+V
- Undo the last action   Ctrl+Z
- Redo the last action   Ctrl+Y

Printing and previewing/views

- Print a document   Ctrl+P
- Print preview   Alt+Ctrl+I
- Print layout view   Alt+Ctrl+P
- Web layout view   Alt+Ctrl+O
- Draft View   Alt+Ctrl+N

Paragraphs

- *Center the Text*   *Ctrl+E*
- *Left-Alignment*   *Ctrl+L*
- *Right-Alignment*   *Ctrl+R*
- *Indent*   *Ctrl+M*
- *Justify*   *Ctrl+J*

Extras

- *Insert today's date*   *Alt+Shift+D*
- *Insert Current Time*   *Alt+Shift+T*
- *Insert Footnote*   *Alt+Ctrl+F*
- *Insert Endnote*   *Alt+Ctrl+D*
- *Insert Comment*   *Ctrl+Alt+M*
- *Open Help*   *F1*
- *Find*   *Ctrl+F*
- *Find/Replace*   *Ctrl+H*
- *Word Count*   *Ctrl+Shift+G*
- *Go to File*   *Alt+F*

Conclusion

Well, that's about it. You should be well on your way to mastering Word 2013 RT. You should now be able to navigate your way around, create some beautiful documents, and share them with the world. You can take a document from a blank slate to a finished masterpiece. You can take a template and truly make it your own. We've shown you the essentials, but more importantly, we've tried to instill in you the confidence to tackle any word processing task that might come your way tomorrow, while allowing you to get things done today.

We sincerely hope you've enjoyed reading this guide as much as we've enjoyed writing it. We're sure that you'll be getting plenty of use Office RT 2013 on your Windows RT tablet for years to come.

Thanks for reading!

About Minute Help Press

Minute Help Press is building a library of books for people with only minutes to spare. Follow @minutehelp on Twitter to receive the latest information about free and paid publications from Minute Help Press, or visit minutehelpguides.com.